From Darkness to Light

Poems on a Christian Pilgrim's Journey

Julius T. Nganji

From Darkness to Light: Poems on a Christian Pilgrim's Journey

Copyright © 2022 Julius T. Nganji

Published by Nganji Publishing
Gatineau (QC), Canada

Nganji.com

All Rights Reserved. No part of this publication may be reproduced, stored in a retrieval system, or transmitted, in any form or in any means – by electronic, mechanical, photocopying, recording or otherwise – without prior written permission.

Cover Design, illustration, and layout: Sikutskido

Unless otherwise indicated, Scripture quotations are from the ESV® Bible (The Holy Bible, English Standard Version®), copyright © 2001 by Crossway, a publishing ministry of Good News Publishers. Used by permission. All rights reserved.

ISBN: 978-1-7782677-1-0 (eBook)
ISBN: 978-1-7782677-0-3 (Paperback)

Library and Archives Canada Legal Deposit: 2022

*For my father, Nsangong Nganji Manasses (of blessed memory),
my mother Rebecca Nganji,
and for all Christians on their journey to heaven
who pass through tough times, trials, and temptations,
but keep their eyes fixed on Jesus Christ.*

Acknowledgements

These poems were written over a few years and first typeset in 2003 but never published. At a time when I did not have access to a personal computer, it was originally typeset by Gilles Nganji. Today, with the ease of self-publishing online, I realise the need to publish them so that others could benefit from the encouragement within.

Since they were written, several people read through and gave feedback which has shaped the way the poems are today. I would like to thank some of them.

I'm grateful to Pastors Mbinglo Koyo Amos, Gabe Barnabas, and Donatus Ngamsiha for their invaluable feedback on the original manuscript and in 2022, they were also reviewed by Dr. Dieudonne Tamfu and Andrew Kenny.

Above all, I give all thanks and glory to God Almighty for the inspiration, strength, saving and sustaining grace. Without Him, I can do nothing.

Table of Contents

Acknowledgements iv
Foreword viii
Section 1: Under Sin's Dominion 1
   Idols! The Folly of It All 2
   Jesus Is Weeping 4
   Jesus The Answer 6
Section 2: Breaking the Yoke of Sin 9
   Lord, Let Me into Heaven 10
   Farewell…Welcome 12
   Freedom in Jesus Christ 14
   A Christian 16
   True Joy 18
   I Want to Praise 20
Section 3: Pain and Suffering on the Journey 23
   The Ministry of Thorns 24
   In the Storm 26
   Conserve Holy Oil 28
   The Issue of Blood 30
Section 4: Battle with the Enemy 33
   Our Warfare 34
   Temptations Are Coming 36
   Weakness of Men Folk 38
   Pray Or Be a Prey 40
   Only By Grace 42
   The Devil Is a Fool 44
   The Promised Land 46
Section 5: Help on the Journey 49
   A Faithful God 50

The Greatest Professor	52
God of Success	53
God's Word	54
Look Unto Jesus	56
Mustard Seed Faith	58
My God Is	60
Tongues of Fire	66
God Will Provide	68
Stronger In Weakness	70
Section 6: Perseverance and Victory	**73**
Work For Your Crown	74
Courage Pilgrim	76
The Joyful Morning Comes	78
Weep Not	80

Foreword

I count it a great privilege to be asked to write a foreword for Dr. Julius T. Nganji's book of poems entitled: 'From Darkness to Light: Poems on a Christian Pilgrim's Journey.'

The title of the book certainly describes well what you can expect to find within it, as it takes the reader along each step of the Christian's journey from the position of being: 'without God and without hope in the world', through facing troubles and trials, to finally reaching its victorious end.

Like Christian, in John Bunyan's 'Pilgrim's Progress, the first section begins with poems by the writer, as one still 'Under Sin's Dominion' and not yet a Christian.

The next section, entitled 'Breaking the Yoke of Sin', has poems when the pilgrim has been set free and started along the Christian journey. The next two sections: 'Pain and Suffering on the Journey', and the 'Battle with the Enemy' are very significant and must always be taken into account when a person decides to become a Christian. As Paul and Barnabas warned their new converts: 'We must go through many hardships to enter the kingdom of God'. Acts 14. 22. There is no point telling people that being a Christian is easy, as they will discover, sooner or later, that they have many enemies, including the world, the flesh, and the devil to contend with.

The next section: 'Help on the Journey' is perfectly placed to encourage and aid the Christian along the path when troubles do come along.

The final section: 'Perseverance and Victory', again encourages the Christian that God will help us persevere and that victory is certain in Christ.

I also love this book as each poem has an appropriate Bible reference attached, showing the reader that the inspiration for these poems is not from man's mere wisdom, but comes from the word of God, and because of this, they can be fully trusted.

The storms of this life may rage,
Hell's host a battle may wage,
God has given dominion,
Only maintain union,
Weeping for the night may tarry,
But joy your sorrow will carry,
In the morning
The glorious morning. (From When the Joyful Morning Comes')

Andrew W. Kenny, M.A., University of Sheffield, England.

Section 1: Under Sin's Dominion

Idols! The Folly of It All

Their idols are silver and gold, the work of human hands. They have mouths, but do not speak; eyes, but do not see. They have ears, but do not hear; noses, but do not smell. They have hands, but do not feel; feet, but do not walk; and they do not make a sound in their throat. Those who make them become like them; so do all who trust in them. **Psalm 115: 4-8**

Idols! The Folly of It All

Can man make a true god?
Some tried out of wood,
And others out of stone,
Worshipping it many years,
Yet remaining in their tears.

Some are tied into beads,
And are called "layas",
These chains are liars,
Worshipping them many years,
Your life becomes a waste.

These idols are scarecrows,
Even a cock crows,
I hate useless gods,
Such gods cannot deliver,
But at thunder sound quiver.

From Darkness to Light

Jesus Is Weeping

And Jesus entered the temple and drove out all who sold and bought in the temple, and he overturned the tables of the money-changers and the seats of those who sold pigeons. He said to them, "It is written, 'My house shall be called a house of prayer,' but you make it a den of robbers." **Matthew 21:12-13**

In His temple, prostitutes
Worshipping their god,
Adding to the destitute,
Stigmatising God's household with their cords.

In His temple, thieves
Doing their business,
Sending out the sheaves,
Saturating God's house with sinfulness.

He says: I paid the price,
But men continue in sin,
He weeps: They spurn my sacrifice,
Veiled to hell's bloody scene.

Jesus The Answer

Behold, I stand at the door and knock. If anyone hears my voice and opens the door, I will come in to him and eat with him, and he with me. **Revelation 3:20**

Are you in sin's pool?
Where there is great doom?
Your desire, sin to eliminate?
Let Jesus come into your room.

Your heart's door He knocks,
You must unlock,
Let Him in by praying,
Or you will be straying.

Section 2: Breaking the Yoke of Sin

Lord, Let Me into Heaven

Open to me the gates of righteousness, that I may enter through them and give thanks to the Lord. This is the gate of the Lord; the righteous shall enter through it. I thank you that you have answered me and have become my salvation.
Psalm 118:19-21

Lord, Let Me into Heaven

My Lord and my God,
I am a sinner
Punish me not with your rod
I need your fellowship

I have found salvation,
Open your door for me
I come with exaltation
Rolling on your floor

Let me in to serve,
Your Highness the King
I will bring what I reserved
And to your true praise sing.

Farewell…Welcome

Now the works of the flesh are evident: sexual immorality, impurity, sensuality, idolatry, sorcery, enmity, strife, jealousy, fits of anger, rivalries, dissensions, divisions, envy, drunkenness, orgies, and things like these. I warn you, as I warned you before, that those who do such things will not inherit the kingdom of God. But the fruit of the Spirit is love, joy, peace, patience, kindness, goodness, faithfulness, gentleness, self-control; against such things there is no law. And those who belong to Christ Jesus have crucified the flesh with its passions and desires.
Galatians 5:19-24

Farewell...Welcome

Farewell, farewell
Fornication, impurity
Debauchery, idolatry
Hatred, jealousy, strife, sorcery
Anger, selfishness
Dissension and factions,
Envy, drunkenness, orgies
Farewell all works of the flesh
I am born again,
No more a natural man.

Welcome, welcome
The Holy Spirit gives me these:
Welcome real love and deep joy,
You are welcome true peace and patience,
Kindness and goodness,
Faithfulness, gentleness,
Yes, welcome fruit of the Spirit
I am born again,
Now a fruitful child of God.

Freedom in Jesus Christ

Jesus answered them, "Truly, truly, I say to you, everyone who practices sin is a slave to sin. The slave does not remain in the house forever; the son remains forever. So if the Son sets you free, you will be free indeed. **John 8:34-36**

Freedom in Jesus Christ

Oh, true freedom,
Is found in God's kingdom,
Freedom from the power of sin,
The world has not seen.

Freedom with peace,
Oh, what masterpiece!
Freedom of the soul,
That cannot be sold.

Freedom in Christ,
There is no other name,
In whom we can trust,
His power is the same.

A Christian

But God, being rich in mercy, because of the great love with which he loved us, even when we were dead in our trespasses, made us alive together with Christ— by grace you have been saved— and raised us up with him and seated us with him in the heavenly places in Christ Jesus. **Ephesians 2:4-6**

A Christian

To be in God is to have life,
It is to live aright,
Fellowshipping in God's light,
And in Him to delight.

It is in God to find favour,
Taste salvation's flavour,
God's fellowship to savour,
Then Satan would not devour.

In God is no such thing as tribes,
None who likes to take sides,
And God's assembly divides,
No one with a god besides.

True Joy

May the God of hope fill you with all joy and peace in believing, so that by the power of the Holy Spirit you may abound in hope. **Romans 15:13**

True Joy

Lord, I want it deeper
Not so shallow, would I desire
For shallowness lasts the twinkling of an eye

I want it like stronger and deeper roots
Sucking and distributing essential nutrients
To the branches, thus bearing attractive fruits

As people are attracted to succulent fruit
So, they are to those with such radiance
That comes from deeper joy and inner peace

I know you alone are the source
Of true joy, unshakable in all circumstances
True peace and joy come from God alone
No, not from what we have or who we are.

I Want to Praise

Praise the Lord! Praise the Lord, O my soul! I will praise the Lord as long as I live; I will sing praises to my God while I have my being. **Psalm 146:1-2**

I Want to Praise

Lord Jesus, fill my heart,
With a wonderful praise,
To quench the devil's dart,
By your wonderful grace.

Fill my heart each morning,
When I rise from sleep
With a fresh mind
To challenge the devil.

Fill my heart each afternoon,
As I go through my activities
With a crowded mind
To say no to Satan.

Fill my heart each evening,
When I retire home
With great satisfaction
And songs of adoration.

On my praise be enthroned,
Let me no more be frail,
Let the devil be dethroned,
And I will no longer derail.

Section 3: Pain and Suffering on the Journey

The Ministry of Thorns

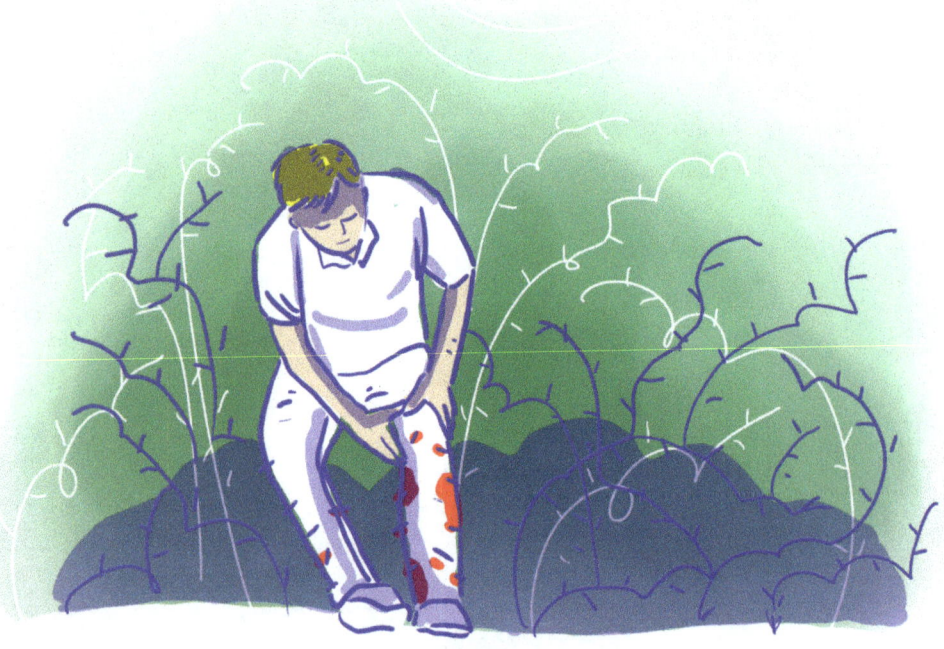

Count it all joy, my brothers, when you meet trials of various kinds, for you know that the testing of your faith produces steadfastness. And let steadfastness have its full effect, that you may be perfect and complete, lacking in nothing.
James 1:2-4

The Ministry of Thorns

Dread not the valley of suffering
Or think in it that God is flattering
Appropriate the spoils therein,
Then you will come out richer than you went in
You are not the first to taste of it.

God did not take away Paul's thorn
Nor showed in it that He was flattering
He made Paul strong therewith within,
Then he came out richer than he was
He is not the last to taste of it.

Dread not the valley of suffering
Or think in it that God is flattering
He makes you strong therewith within,
And shows His worth in a ministry of thorns
You are not exempt to taste of it.

In the Storm

When you pass through the waters, I will be with you; and through the rivers, they shall not overwhelm you; when you walk through fire you shall not be burned, and the flame shall not consume you. **Isaiah 43:2**

In the Storm

Flee not from the storm,
Therein is your Christ awaiting,
To give you a new form,
He takes away your mortal flesh,
To give you a new form,
Flee not from the storm.

Flee not from the storm,
Therein is a mold for you,
To mold you up to maturity,
Therein is refining fire,
To refine you as pure gold,
Flee not from the storm.

Conserve Holy Oil

Blessed be the God and Father of our Lord Jesus Christ, the Father of mercies and God of all comfort, who comforts us in all our affliction, so that we may be able to comfort those who are in any affliction, with the comfort with which we ourselves are comforted by God. **2 Corinthians 1:3-4**

Conserve Holy Oil

Spill not your oil,
Conserve your oil,
The precious oil of your suffering,
That weary pilgrim needs it.

Despise not your oil,
Gold cannot purchase it,
Save one who passed through,
And harvested much.

Spare not your toil,
Share of your oil,
Into the rusted gates,
To save others from their toil.

From Darkness to Light

The Issue of Blood

And there was a woman who had had a discharge of blood for twelve years, and though she had spent all her living on physicians, she could not be healed by anyone. She came up behind him and touched the fringe of his garment, and immediately her discharge of blood ceased. **Luke 8:43-44**

The Issue of Blood

Twelve years of agony,
Twelve years disharmony,
Twelve years of trying,
To stop the flood of blood.

Twelve years in seclusion,
Twelve years in poverty,
Twelve years in sickness,
Not a penny was left.

Twelve years of consultation,
Twelve years of fruitlessness,
Twelve years of Christ searching,
Then came the Christ.

Great day in her life,
Great day of health restoration,
Wrinkles disappearing from her face,
Once in twelve years.

Section 4: Battle with the Enemy

Our Warfare

Finally, be strong in the Lord and in the strength of his might. Put on the whole armor of God, that you may be able to stand against the schemes of the devil. For we do not wrestle against flesh and blood, but against the rulers, against the authorities, against the cosmic powers over this present darkness, against the spiritual forces of evil in the heavenly places. **Ephesians 6:10-12**

Our Warfare

Oh, sinner man Jesus knocks,
Just at the door of your heart,
But the devil warns,
With a courage so evil,
And strength like the weevil's,
But Almighty can scatter barns.

Now that you are in Jesus Christ,
Satan sends host of demons,
At you they shake fists,
Exalting their king mammon,
To distract you from Christ,
And make you a man so common.

Oh he may try to sink you,
In those pools of worldliness,
God makes a way through,
Because of His worthiness,
And His omnipotence,
He is able to carry you through.

Never be afraid God's son,
Although the devil frightens,
You to imprison,
Our accuser threatens,
To harm if you hearken,
To your master Jesus; God's son.

Temptations Are Coming

Therefore let anyone who thinks that he stands take heed lest he fall. No temptation has overtaken you that is not common to man. God is faithful, and he will not let you be tempted beyond your ability, but with the temptation he will also provide the way of escape, that you may be able to endure it.**1 Corinthians 10:12-13**

Temptations Are Coming

An awful sound I hear,
Like a tempestuous wind,
In readiness to tear,
Weak men in battle ring.

May you men gird your loins,
And let temptations flee,
All that temptation coins,
Will not offend you.

They surround and hover,
Let God's armour cover,
Bind their necks and their legs,
Then rejoice over their remains.

From Darkness to Light

Weakness of Men Folk

And David sent and inquired about the woman. And one said, "Is not this Bathsheba, the daughter of Eliam, the wife of Uriah the Hittite?" So David sent messengers and took her, and she came to him, and he lay with her. (Now she had been purifying herself from her uncleanness.) Then she returned to her house. And the woman conceived, and she sent and told David, "I am pregnant."
2 Samuel 11:3-5

David,
> It is not Goliath,
> That quenches your fire,
> But your desire,
> Your thrust of lust.

Believer,
> You might lack such action,
> Perhaps such thoughts,
> Splitting peace with God,
> Till your morale rots.

Bind such thoughts,
> Refuse that ration,
> And devilish actions,
> Find peace in godly thoughts.

Pray Or Be a Prey

And he came to the disciples and found them sleeping. And he said to Peter, "So, could you not watch with me one hour? Watch and pray that you may not enter into temptation. The spirit indeed is willing, but the flesh is weak." **Matthew 26:40-41**

On your walls, O Jerusalem, I have set watchmen; all the day and all the night they shall never be silent. You who put the Lord in remembrance, take no rest, and give him no rest until he establishes Jerusalem and makes it a praise in the earth. **Isaiah 62:6-7**

Pray or be a prey,
To the roaring lion,
Unworthy to ascend,
The holy mount Zion.

Peter did not pray,
So, he became a prey,
At refusal, he wept,
Because commandment was not kept.

Try hard to stay,
Take heed not to stray,
Christ wants you to tarry,
Your burden He would carry.

Try to insist,
Make sure you persist,
Give God no rest,
Till He gives you the best.

Only By Grace

For by grace you have been saved through faith. And this is not your own doing; it is the gift of God, not a result of works, so that no one may boast. **Ephesians 2:8-9**

Mortal man
Why do you boast
When used by God
To accomplish great things?

It is His grace in you
That enables you to serve Him
Without which you are a tiny worm
With no power of your own

Why compel your followers
To call you all the world's titles
For your ego's sake
When Master Jesus should be your model?

Never did he delight in glorifying himself
Rather, did he do all for His father
He humbled himself in all he did
And was lifted by the one who gave the mission

Next time when pride shows up
Servant of God, remember Nebuchadnezzar
And all who did not give him the glory
Shudder with fear and give him the glory.

From Darkness to Light

The Devil Is a Fool

And the beast was captured, and with it the false prophet who in its presence had done the signs by which he deceived those who had received the mark of the beast and those who worshiped its image. These two were thrown alive into the lake of fire that burns with sulfur. **Revelation 19:20**

The devil is a fool
He cannot stop God's love
I love Christ the gentle dove
Who gives salvation,

The devil is jealous
He wants to destroy God's word
He hates people so zealous
Who take up the sword,

The devil is so dull
He shall be totally crushed
His reign shall finally fall
To hell he will be rushed

The devil is a big fool
The battle he has lost
He considers not the cost
To challenge God's rule.

The Promised Land

You shall surely destroy all the places where the nations whom you shall dispossess served their gods, on the high mountains and on the hills and under every green tree. You shall tear down their altars and dash in pieces their pillars and burn their Asherim with fire. You shall chop down the carved images of their gods and destroy their name out of that place. You shall not worship the Lord your God in that way. **Deuteronomy 12:2-4**

The Promised Land

Possession of that great land,
Is through the wilderness,
Your worn-out feet must tread its sand,
Your soul thirst, because of dryness.

Dispossess the Jebusites,
Destroy the Amorites,
Discourage the Anakims,
And all that stand your way.

Put on God's full armour,
To quench all fiery darts,
Fear not the Jericho clamour,
For in that land, you will chat.

Section 5: Help on the Journey

From Darkness to Light

A Faithful God

The saying is trustworthy, for: If we have died with him, we will also live with him; if we endure, we will also reign with him; if we deny him, he also will deny us; if we are faithless, he remains faithful— for he cannot deny himself. **2 Timothy 2:11-13**

A Faithful God

His great faithfulness puzzles me,
It remains unshaken,
Jehovah's greatness I see,
His path I have taken.

Men desire to be prayerful,
Satan presents sweet sleep,
God's morning call is wonderful,
Echoing in sleep so deep.

Men desire to turn from sin,
With God's Spirit they are sealed,
Many temptations they see,
Each blessed day He fills them.

The Greatest Professor

And they were astonished at his teaching, for he taught them as one who had authority, and not as the scribes. **Mark 1:22**

The Greatest Professor

He never went to school,
Don't think Him a fool,
He was greatly honoured,
As He taught professors.

Never been to a medical school,
But with healing power full,
Never been to a rabbinical school,
But Jesus taught even rabbis!

From Darkness to Light

God of Success

And the Lord will make you the head and not the tail, and you shall only go up and not down, if you obey the commandments of the Lord your God, which I command you today, being careful to do them, and if you do not turn aside from any of the words that I command you today, to the right hand or to the left, to go after other gods to serve them. **Deuteronomy 28:13-14**

King Jesus is the Head,
I will not fail,
Though I see the storm ahead,
By His grace, I will prevail.

My soul greatly thirsts,
For his word daily,
That effectively equips me,
For whatever lies ahead.

I love His Excellency,
My great Engineer,
Discouragement seeks to prevail,
But encouragement, He is the pioneer.

King Jesus is the Head,
I will not fail,
Even through the storm ahead,
I will continue to prevail.

From Darkness to Light

God's Word

How sweet are your words to my taste, sweeter than honey to my mouth! Through your precepts I get understanding; therefore I hate every false way. Your word is a lamp to my feet and a light to my path. **Psalm 119:103-105**

God's Word

Sweet, sweet, sweet
Sweeter than pure honey,
Richer than all our gold,
God's word nourishes so sweet.

Sharp, sharp, sharp
Sharper than two-edged sword,
God has an instructing word,
Why not praise Him with grace!

Light, light, light
Unto the feet a lamp,
And unto my path a light,
Leading safely to God.

From Darkness to Light

Look Unto Jesus

Therefore, since we are surrounded by so great a cloud of witnesses, let us also lay aside every weight, and sin which clings so closely, and let us run with endurance the race that is set before us, looking to Jesus, the founder and perfecter of our faith, who for the joy that was set before him endured the cross, despising the shame, and is seated at the right hand of the throne of God. **Romans 12: 1-2**

Look Unto Jesus

As on life's boat you sail,
Sailing in life's boat so frail,
Dwell not on this life's frailty,
Or from Christ you will derail

Life's full of weaknesses,
Where God's power is perfected,
Yours might be frequent illnesses,
God's power would still be respected

Keep looking unto Jesus,
Trusting in His power to save
Keep looking unto Jesus,
Letting Him reign supreme.

Mustard Seed Faith

Now faith is the assurance of things hoped for, the conviction of things not seen. For by it the people of old received their commendation. By faith we understand that the universe was created by the word of God, so that what is seen was not made out of things that are visible. **Hebrews 11:1-3**

Mustard Seed Faith

Faith has no need for an umbrella,
In the heart of the rainy season,
But greatly needs a strong umbrella,
In the heart of the dry season,
After a sincere prayer with sweet-smelling savour,
To seek God's favour.

Faith passes an examination,
But seriously embarks on the studying process,
Then she goes to confirm her success,
On the day of examination,
Oh! There is nothing too difficult for faith,
The mustard seed faith.

My God Is ...

Lift up your heads, O gates! And be lifted up, O ancient doors, that the King of glory may come in. Who is this King of glory? The Lord, strong and mighty, the Lord, mighty in battle! Lift up your heads, O gates! And lift them up, O ancient

My God Is …

doors, that the King of glory may come in. Who is this King of glory? The Lord of hosts, he is the King of glory! Selah. **Psalm 24:7-10**

The only Author of true love,
Whose pure love knows no limit,
His only begotten, sent He
In your place to die.

So merciful and gracious,
He off loads sins and gives rest,
As far as the East is from the West,
Separates He sins from His precious.

The greatest one who rescues,
All honour to Him is due,
Judah's Lion snatches into hands,
His people from roaring lion's fangs.

The greatest one who nurtures,
More than a nursing mother,
Gospel milk nurtures until rapture,
No devil-antigen can bother.

The caring God one should seek,
Mother hen cares for chicks,
God gathers them under wings' shadow,
Covering the righteous with great tower.

The greatest physician,
In sickness hard, he deals
Witch doctors have tried, even clinicians
Only Great Jehovah heals.

A mighty man in battle,
Whole armour's good, says history
Unto offensive fight they rattle,
El Shaddai gives victory.

My God Is ...

A righteous and perfect judge,
He Knows not partiality,
His wonderful judgement none will dodge,
He uses justice and equity.

Rewarder of excellence,
Back to the world He comes,
To condemn all decadence,
Everyone reaps what he sows.

The greatest who inspires,
Books have not all about Him,
I decide a minute to retire,
As the devil escape to his realm.

From Darkness to Light

Tongues of Fire

When the day of Pentecost arrived, they were all together in one place. And suddenly there came from heaven a sound like a mighty rushing wind, and it filled the entire house where they were sitting. And divided tongues as of fire appeared to them and rested on each one of them. And they were all filled with the Holy Spirit and began to speak in other tongues as the Spirit gave them utterance.
Acts 2:1-4

When God's children need bread,
He gives them no stone,
It is His goodwill,
To fill His children
With His Holy Spirit,
Equipping them for service
Would you be void of such power?
Come and be anointed for service.

God Will Provide

Do not be anxious about anything, but in everything by prayer and supplication with thanksgiving let your requests be made known to God. And the peace of God, which surpasses all understanding, will guard your hearts and your minds in Christ Jesus. **Philippians 4:6-7**

God Will Provide

I may not know
Where my next meal will come from
In what quality or quantity
But this I know
The one who feeds the birds, will feed me

I may not know
Where I will get clothing
Whether it will be good enough to keep me warm
But this I know
The one who clothes the lilies, will clothe me

Rather than worry
About my next meal or clothing
This will I do
Trust in Jehovah Jireh
For He will supply all my needs according to his riches.

From Darkness to Light

Stronger In Weakness

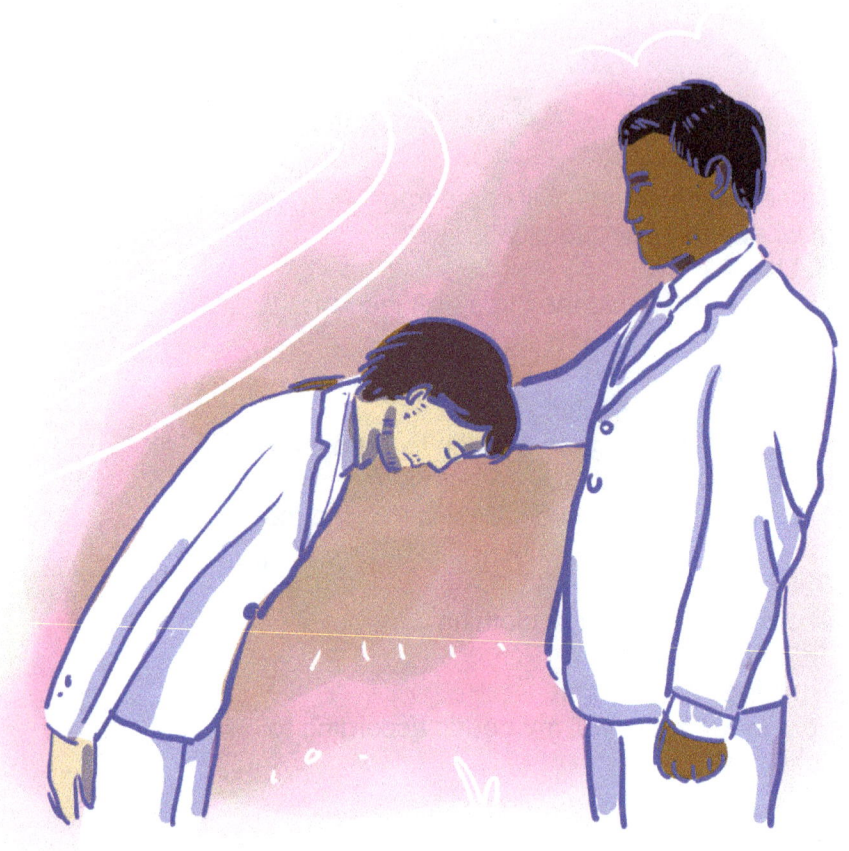

So to keep me from becoming conceited because of the surpassing greatness of the revelations, a thorn was given me in the flesh, a messenger of Satan to harass me, to keep me from becoming conceited. Three times I pleaded with the Lord about this, that it should leave me. But he said to me, "My grace is sufficient for you, for my power is made perfect in weakness." Therefore I will boast all the more gladly of my weaknesses, so that the power of Christ may rest upon me. For the sake of Christ, then, I am content with weaknesses, insults, hardships, persecutions, and calamities. For when I am weak, then I am strong. **2 Corinthians 12: 7-10**

Stronger In Weakness

Lord, I do not understand all your ways
Your rationale for choosing certain things
How can we be stronger in weakness,
It is contrary to our culture

Your strength Oh Lord
Is made perfect, perfect in weakness
When we are weak, then we are strong
Your wisdom is foolishness to the world

You call weak folks who cannot speak
And use them to do great things
When they acknowledge their frailty
And depend on you alone

Oh Lord, you bypass the proud and arrogant
Who depend on their strength and ego,
You dwell with those broken in spirit and contrite in heart
Your heart connects with theirs; you do not despise such

When I cannot speak boldly
Or argue as the world demands
I will like a child, depend on you, my Father
Whose strength is made perfect in my weakness.

Section 6: Perseverance and Victory

Work For Your Crown

Therefore, my beloved, as you have always obeyed, so now, not only as in my presence but much more in my absence, work out your own salvation with fear and trembling, for it is God who works in you, both to will and to work for his good pleasure. **Philippians 2:12-13**

Work For Your Crown

No man, to receive any crown
Is not walking amongst the lilies,
Or plains without obstacles,
But on rocky mountains and valleys,
For no suffering, no crown.

The mighty conqueror of war,
Many sounds of the bullet must hear,
And its pains in battle fear,
But after the victory comes the crown,
For no suffering, no crown.

Students must burn night candles,
And a mastery of subject handle,
Then would come the good success,
And then the crown of great success,
For no suffering, no crown.

Christians must face persecutions,
And expect from kinsmen rejections,
Not fearing executions,
But thereafter comes the great crown,
For no suffering, no crown.

From Darkness to Light

Courage Pilgrim

And let us not grow weary of doing good, for in due season we will reap, if we do not give up. So then, as we have opportunity, let us do good to everyone, and especially to those who are of the household of faith. **Galatians 6:9-10**

Courage Pilgrim

Take heart weary pilgrim,
Do not give it up,
Your Saviour knows,
How you feel
And he will bear you up.

A stone-throw to glory,
Do not give it up,
The heavenlies,
Are waiting,
And they will bear you in.

Why would you faint,
Just at the gate,
Of your final abode?
There the king awaits,
Like a receptionist.

The Joyful Morning Comes

O Lord, you have brought up my soul from Sheol; you restored me to life from among those who go down to the pit. Sing praises to the Lord, O you his saints, and give thanks to his holy name. For his anger is but for a moment, and his favor is for a lifetime. Weeping may tarry for the night, but joy comes with the morning. **Psalm 30:3-5**

The Joyful Morning Comes

Weary soul, does no one care,
And your burdens alone bear?
Are you laden with distress,
And life full of sickness?
Weeping for the night may tarry,
But joy your sorrow will carry,
In the morning
The peaceful morning

The day in tiredness frowns,
And the awful night it crowns.
Childbirth may increase its pangs,
And sharpen its long fangs,
Weeping for the night may tarry,
But joy your sorrow will carry,
In the morning
The joyful morning

The storms of this life may rage,
Hell's host a battle may wage,
God has given dominion,
Only maintain union,
Weeping for the night may tarry,
But joy your sorrow will carry,
In the morning
The glorious morning.

From Darkness to Light

Weep Not

For the Lord himself will descend from heaven with a cry of command, with the voice of an archangel, and with the sound of the trumpet of God. And the dead in Christ will rise first. Then we who are alive, who are left, will be caught up together with them in the clouds to meet the Lord in the air, and so we will always be with the Lord. Therefore encourage one another with these words. **1 Thessalonians 4:16-18**

Weep Not

If I should die,
Weep not hopelessly
Laugh not mercilessly,
For to heaven, I will fly.

Many people live daily, seeking to fill a void within. In seeking the numerous pleasures of this world, some are held captive in the pool of sin. Thankfully, God sent his one and only son Jesus Christ to rescue us and fill that void.

For those who by God's grace learn to trust and depend on Jesus, true joy, peace, and satisfaction is theirs. On their journey towards God the Father, they will face numerous challenges, but are assured of God's help. They will never be forsaken, even though when the storms of life rage, it often feels as if God has forsaken them.

"Come to me, all who labor and are heavy laden, and I will give you rest." **Matthew 11:28.**

When inspired, Julius T. Nganji loves to write poems, plays and short stories that glorify God. He currently lives in Gatineau, Canada with his wife Gloria and two sons Nathan and Samuel.

www.ingramcontent.com/pod-product-compliance
Lightning Source LLC
Chambersburg PA
CBHW060211050426
42446CB00013B/3044